Navigating WebCT

A Student's Guide

M. E. Sokolik, Ph.D.

University of California, Berkeley

Prentice
Hall

Upper Saddle River, New Jersey 07458

Acquisitions Editor: Alison Pendergast
Managing Editor: Judy Leale
Interior Design: Michael Fruhbeis
Cover Design: Stacey Abraham
Associate Director, Multimedia Production: Karen Goldsmith
Manager, Print Production: Christy Mahon
Manufacturing Buyer: Wanda Rockwell
Printer/Binder: Victor Graphics, Inc.

Credits and acknowledgments borrowed from other sources and reproduced, with permission, in this textbook appear on appropriate page within text.

Prentice Hall

ISBN 0-13-100284-8

10 9 8 7 6 5

Contents

Module 1 — Introduction to the World Wide Web and WebCT

About the Internet

In the early 1960's, with the threat of nuclear war, the Department of Defense began to develop a global communication system. In conjunction with several universities, an interconnected network known as the Internet was established to relay text messages. Early on, educational institutions realized the power of the Internet. College and university faculty members began collaborating on projects through the Internet, and email and document sharing between faculty and students became commonplace. Yet there were limitations. Only basic text messages could travel over the Internet. It could not handle graphics, audio, or video.

The creation of the World Wide Web (commonly known as the Web) in the mid-1990s provided a means to display rich multimedia content on the Internet through the use of a Web browser. A Web browser is a graphical user interface (GUI), which is a computer program that interprets hypertext computer code to display material—graphics and text—on the screen. With a browser, a user can work with plug-ins, which are programs that provide audio and video. A browser also links the power of the Internet with other computer programs to open up collaboration and communication in a variety of formats. And with a browser a user can move from site to site with a click of a mouse, instead of having to type in an exact Internet address.

The popularity of the Internet is worldwide. Millions of people interact with one another on a daily basis, sharing ideas and discussing issues through the freedom of open communication. Remember that when you are using the Internet, your computer is connected to other computers. The WebCT course you are participating in is located on another machine on the Internet, and you are accessing that machine through your Web browser. Many people and machines must work together to have the Internet run smoothly.

What Is WebCT?

WebCT—shorthand for "Web Course Tools"—is a browser-based course management system that delivers course materials and enables class interaction. In fact, WebCT is a collection of different tools that allows you to submit homework, take quizzes, read course

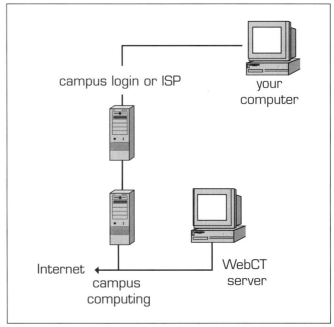

Figure 1.1 Example of Connection to WebCT and the Internet

materials, receive comments and grades from your instructors, communicate with classmates and your instructor, and more. Which of these tools you will use depends on which tools your instructors have chosen to integrate into your courses. You can find out more about WebCT and what it can do at **http://www.webct.com**.

Learning with a Course Management System

You may be new to using an online course management system, or perhaps you have had previous experience. In either case, here is a checklist to help you become a better learner in an online environment.

✔ **Take time to familiarize yourself with the website for your course.** Find out the course schedule, the course requirements, the method for contacting your instructor, the location of any help files, and so on.

✔ **Review any informational files within your course, and experiment with the navigation.** Try the different links to see where they go. (No, you won't destroy anything by doing this!)

✔ **Log in to the course site regularly.** Look for announcements or updates to the course, which will be posted on your *myWebCT* page (see page 10 for further information). You may also see announcements on the course homepage or on the calendar. Be sure to log in to check your course homepage often.

✔ **Participate in the activities that have been included in your course—online discussions, chat sessions, and so on.** These activities are part of your complete classroom experience.

✔ **Contact your instructor (or whomever your instructor has appointed) whenever you have questions or problems with WebCT.** You can also post questions to your class discussion area. Your classmates may answer you before your instructor does.

✔ **Plan for deadlines.** Computers are less forgiving than your instructor. And keep in mind that the WebCT server you are connecting to may not be in the same time zone as you are. The page that contains the quizzes will also display the current time, as

Tip

Links on the Web require only one click. If you double-click, as you might in other programs, you may cause your browser to slow down because you are issuing multiple commands.

known by the server. If that time differs from your area, please take that into account when planning for due dates.

✔ **Remember that your online course is a public place.** Speak and behave with the same politeness and respect expected in any classroom. (If you find you've posted something that embarrasses you or that gives the wrong impression, ask your instructor to remove it from the course site.)

You can always go to the following address for further information about learning effectively with WebCT:

http://www.webct.com/students

Module 2 Using Your Computer with WebCT

Computer Requirements

The best way to determine the computer system that you will need is to consult your school's computer information page. Different schools run different versions of WebCT, each with slightly different computer requirements. This guide generally assumes that you are using version 3.6 or 3.7, the most recent campus editions of WebCT. The following *minimum* basic setups should work with most versions of WebCT.

✔ **IBM/PC compatible.** 100 MHz processor with at least 32 MB of memory and 16 MB of free space on the hard drive and a monitor. Depending on the types of files in your course, you may also need a sound card and speakers or headphones. Operating systems: Windows 98 or higher, NT 4.0, or any Linux 2. You will need a modem (28.8K or better) or network card and a connection to the Internet.

✔ **Apple Macintosh.** Power PC (preferably a G3 or G4) with at least 32 MB of memory and 10 MB of free space on the hard drive and a monitor. Depending on the types of files in your course, you may also need audio speakers or headphones. Operating systems: 7.5 or higher, or any Linux 2. In OS 7.x, 8.x, and 9.x, you should allocate at least 24 MB of your computer's memory to your browser. (In OS X, this is automatically taken care of.) You will need a modem (28.8K or better) or network connection to the Internet.

Choosing a Browser

The most popular browsers are Netscape and Microsoft's Internet Explorer. To determine if the version of WebCT your school is using supports your browser, go to the browser tune-up page on WebCT.com.

```
http://www.webct.com/quickstart/viewpage?name
=exchange_browser_tuneup
```

Browser Settings

You should check your browser to make sure that its settings are correct for WebCT. An easy way to do this is with the browser tune-up we just mentioned. Or you can manually adjust your browser settings as follows.

✔ **Step 1. Enable Java**

In Netscape Communicator (Navigator 4.5 and higher)

- select **Edit** → **Preferences**
- select **Advanced**
- make sure the **Enable Java** and **Enable JavaScript** boxes are checked
- click **OK**

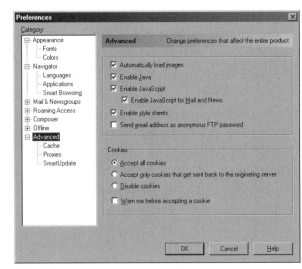

FIGURE 2.1   NETSCAPE COMMUNICATOR JAVA SETTINGS

In Internet Explorer 5.0 and higher

- select **Tools** → **Internet Options**
- select the **Advanced** tab
- locate **Microsoft VM**
- make sure the **Java console enabled** (requires restart) and **Java logging enabled** boxes are checked
- click **OK**
- restart your computer if you checked the **Java console enabled** box

✔ **Step 2. Set your browser cache to always reload a page**

In Netscape Communicator (Navigator 4.5 and higher)

- select **Edit** → **Preferences**
- click the + sign next to **Advanced** to see more options
- select **Cache**
- select the **Every Time** button at the bottom
- click **OK**

In Internet Explorer 5.0 and higher

- select **Tools** → **Internet Options**
- select the **General** tab
- select **Settings** from Temporary Internet Files
- select the **Every Visit to the Page** button
- click **OK**

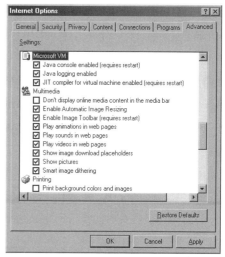

FIGURE 2.2   INTERNET EXPLORER JAVA SETTINGS

✔ **Step 3. Turn off anonymous logon**

In Internet Explorer 5.0 and higher

- select **Tools** → **Internet Options**
- select the **Security** tab
- select **Custom level**
- scroll down to **User Authentication** settings
- **Logon** options
- select the **Automatic logon only in Intranet zone** radio button
- click **OK**

Special Plug-ins

Check with your instructor to learn if there are any plug-ins that you will need to receive course files. You can find out if your browser has these plug-ins by going to the "test drive" area of WebCT at the browser tune-up Internet address provided earlier. Typically, if your browser encounters a file it cannot read, it will prompt you to download and install the plug-in and provide links to the plug-in software.

Module 3 Accessing Your Course and Using *MyWebCT*

Finding Your Course

Your instructor or institution will give you an Internet address, or URL (uniform resource locator), where you will find your course. Launch your browser and enter the appropriate address in the box at the top, as shown in the accompanying illustration.

FIGURE 3.1 ADDRESS BOX ILLUSTRATION

Logins, Passwords, and Access Codes

There are many different ways to set up and log in to WebCT. Most likely, your instructor will provide you with instructions on how to set up and log in to your WebCT account. Follow them carefully, and let your instructor know if you have any difficulties. The following website may help with logging in:

**http://www.webct.com/content/viewpage?name
=support_quickstep_graphic**

If your course requires an access code, a new screen will ask you to enter that information. Access codes may be purchased online at **www.webct.com**, bundled with your textbook, or sold as a stand-alone package from your campus bookstore. Please ensure that you enter the access code exactly as it appears (including punctuation). Also, your textbook may be bundled with more than one access code; some of these access codes may be for products other than WebCT, so be careful to enter the correct one. More information on access codes may be found at:

http://www.webct.com/accesscodes/

MyWebCT

Tip

If your instructor has indicated that you must create your own WebCT ID, remember that it will appear when you use different parts of the WebCT program, such as *Chat* and the *Discussions*, and in your instructor's records. It is a good idea to choose a login name that will clearly identify you and does you no harm. "CuteBunny" or "LazyGuy" are probably not good choices.

If your account has not been set up for you, then on your first visit you may need to create a login name and password for yourself using *myWebCT*. *MyWebCT* will give you access to all of your WebCT courses on the server. It may also provide links to

✔ New course content, such as quizzes or discussion postings
✔ Announcements from your school
✔ Internet bookmarks
✔ WebCT.com

If you are taking courses located on only one WebCT server, you need to create a *myWebCT* only once. However, if you are taking courses that are hosted on different servers, you may have to create a *myWebCT* profile on each server. If you aren't sure, check with your instructors about where your courses are located.

✔ **Step 1.** From the WebCT entry page, click **Create *myWebCT***. The *Create myWebCT* page appears.
✔ **Step 2.** Follow the instructions. Complete every field marked with a required asterisk (*).

✔ **Step 3.** Record your WebCT ID and password and keep it in a safe place.

✔ **Step 4.** Click **Continue**.

ADDING A COURSE THAT ALLOWS SELF-REGISTRATION

As mentioned previously, different schools have different ways for students to add courses. If a school allows you to add courses on your own, follow this procedure.

✔ From *myWebCT*, click **Add Course**. The *Course Listing* screen appears, displaying all courses not currently listed in *myWebCT*.

✔ If your school has categories set up, click a category name to view the courses under that category. Find the self-registration course you wish to add, and then click the course name. The *Add a Course to myWebCT* screen appears.

✔ Click **Register**. The *Course Added* screen appears, and the course has been added to *myWebCT*. You can either

• go to the course
• add another course
• return to *myWebCT*

FIGURE 3.2   EXAMPLE OF A WebCT ENTRY PAGE

ADDING A COURSE USING A USER NAME AND PASSWORD

Use this option only if your instructor or school has given you a login name and password. You must also have a user name and password supplied by your school to add a course that does not allow self-registration. If you do not have the required user name and password, contact your instructor about how to get this information.

✔ From *myWebCT*, click **Add Course**. The *Course Listing* screen appears, displaying all courses not currently listed in *myWebCT*.

✔ Click a Category name to view the courses under that category. Find the course you wish to add, and then click the course name. The *Add a Course to myWebCT* screen appears.

✔ Enter the user name and password that your school has given you, and then click **Continue**. The *Course Added* screen appears, and the course has been added to *myWebCT*. You can either

• go to the course
• add another course
• return to *myWebCT*

✔ From now on use your WebCT ID and password to access your WebCT courses.

Accessing a Course from *MyWebCT*

From *myWebCT*, click the name of the course you wish to access. The course homepage appears. Your instructor may have adopted a course called an e-Pack, which is a WebCT course created by a publisher. Some of these courses require an access code. If so, you will be presented with a screen that says "Access Code Required" the first time you attempt to access the course. An access code may be purchased the following three ways:

✔ In a specially marked bundle with your textbook (Be sure that you purchase a book that includes a WebCT access code; some book bundles contain codes for other products.)
✔ As a stand-alone package from your bookstore
✔ By secure online purchase at **http://www.webct.com/accesscodes**

If this course contains e-Pack content, such as that included with one of your textbooks, and this is your first time accessing the course, you may be prompted to enter an access code.

After you enter the access code once, you will be given access to the course materials and will not have to enter it again.

In general, follow your instructor's directions.

Removing a Course from *MyWebCT*

If you no are longer participating in a course or no longer have access to it, you may want to remove it from the *myWebCT* screen. (This option may not always be available.)

✔ From *myWebCT*, click **Remove Course**. The *Remove Course* screen appears, displaying all courses currently listed in *myWebCT*.
✔ Select the course you wish to remove, and then click **Remove**. The course is removed from *myWebCT*.

Removing a course is a permanent choice. Be sure that you really need to delete the course before you proceed.

> **Tip**
>
> Some browsers will allow you to store your login name and password. If you have your own computer and you are the only one who uses it, it will save you time to store your login and password information. If you use a computer in a laboratory or share a computer with others, it is best not to store this information on the computer, as others will have access to your courses using your name.

Viewing Course News

Some courses provide information on the *myWebCT* page about your assignments and for your calendar. You may read "You have new mail" below the appropriate course description on the *myWebCT* page when new mail arrives. Click on this link, and you'll move directly to the mail tool.

You also may a see "There are new quizzes (or discussions, assignments, and so on) available now"

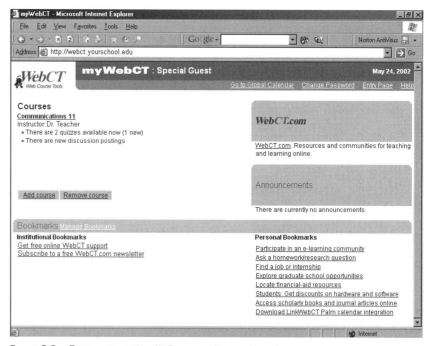

FIGURE 3.3   EXAMPLE OF *MYWEBCT* PAGE WITH COURSE NEWS LISTED

and clicking on this link takes you to the appropriate tool. "You have new grades" tells you your instructor has marked some of your work. It's important to know, however, that clicking on these links to go directly to the new material will not count as a login in the tracking pages (See Chapter 9, page 57 about tracking.). If your instructor keeps track of the number of logins you make, be sure to enter the course by clicking on the course's name to ensure your entry is tracked, and then go to the area with new material.

Passwords

CHANGING YOUR PASSWORD

Depending on the WebCT settings created by your school, this feature may not be available to you. (And although you may be able to change your password, you cannot change your WebCT ID.) Follow these steps to change your password if you need to and if your school allows it.

✔ From *myWebCT*, click **Change Password**. The *Change Password* screen appears.

✔ Complete the text boxes, and then click **Update password**. The *Change Password* confirmation screen appears, and your password is changed.

✔ Click **Continue**. The *Log on to WebCT* screen appears.

✔ In the *WebCT ID* text box, enter your WebCT ID, and in the *Password* text box, enter your new password.

✔ Click **Log on** and *myWebCT* appears.

USING THE LOGON HINT

If you forget your password, use the logon hint you provided when you created your WcbCT ID (if this option is available at your institution).

✔ From the *WebCT* Entry Page, click the **Forgot your password?** link. The *Password Help* screen appears.

✔ In the *WebCT ID* text box, enter your WebCT ID, and then click Go. Your logon hint question appears.

✔ In the *Your Answer* text box, enter the answer to your logon hint question, and then click **Go**. The confirmation screen appears.

✔ Your password is changed, and the new password will be emailed to your registered email account. Click **Continue**. The *WebCT Entry Page* appears.

✔ Retrieve the email containing your new password.

Using your new password, log on to *myWebCT* .

CHANGING THE LOGON HINT

✔ From *myWebCT*, click the **Change Logon Hint** link. The *myWebCT Logon Hint* screen appears.

✔ Follow the on-screen instructions. You must complete all the fields.

✔ Click **Go**. The *Change Logon Hint* confirmation screen appears, and your logon hint is changed.

Bookmarks

MyWebCT displays two types of bookmarked URLs. Your school's WebCT administrator creates institutional bookmarks, and you can also add personal bookmarks. Here's how you can work with both institutional and personal bookmarks.

From *myWebCT*, click **Manage Bookmarks**. The *Bookmarks* screen appears with the institutional bookmarks listed on the left and the personal bookmarks on the right. You can take all the following steps from the *Manage Bookmarks* screen.

✔ Select the bookmark you want to move, and then click either **move up** or **move down**. The bookmark is moved one position. **Note:** You can move only one bookmark at a time.

✔ If you want to hide a bookmark, select it and then click **hide/reveal**. The bookmark is marked "(hidden)".

✔ If you want to reveal a hidden bookmark, select it and then click **hide/reveal**. The bookmark is no longer marked "(hidden)".

To Add Personal Bookmarks

✔ Click **Add Bookmark**. The *Links* page appears.

✔ In the *Name* text box, enter a name for your bookmark. This name will be the link displayed in the *Personal Bookmarks* area.

✔ In the *Location* text box, enter the URL for your bookmark, including the http:// command.

✔ Click **Add Bookmark**. The *Bookmarks* screen appears, displaying your new bookmark.

To Delete Personal Bookmarks

✔ Select the bookmark that you want to delete, and then click **Delete Bookmark**. The bookmark is deleted. **Note:** You can delete multiple bookmarks.

To Edit Personal Bookmarks

✔ Select the bookmark that you want to edit, and then click **Edit Bookmark**. The *Links* screen appears.

✔ Make your changes, and then click **Update Bookmark**. The *Bookmarks* screen appears, displaying your edited bookmark.

When you are finished managing your bookmarks, press **return to WebCT** to view your changes.

Global Calendar

Depending on the configu-
ration of WebCT, the
myWebCT page may have a
link to a calendar for all of
your courses. Use the link
"Go to global calendar" to
reach this page. You can
customize this calendar by
following the on-screen
directions.

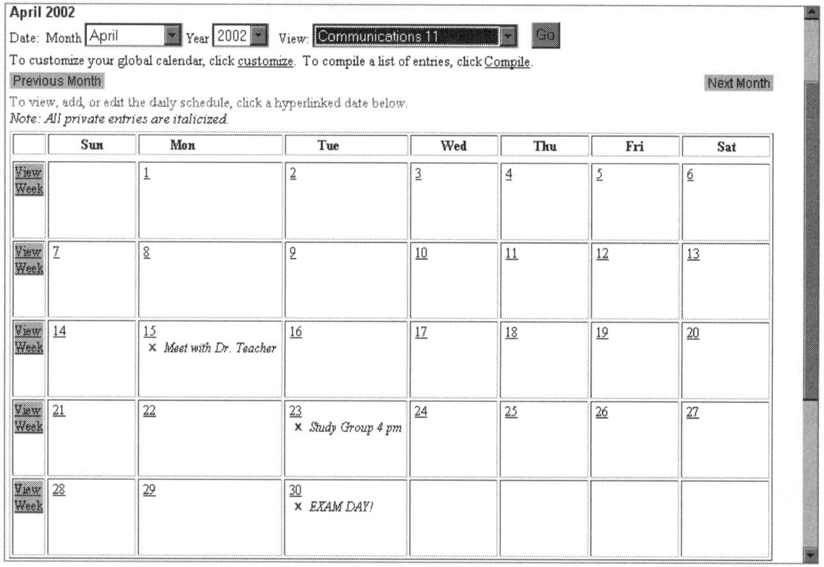

WebCT.com

FIGURE 3-4   EXAMPLE OF A GLOBAL CALENDAR, WITH ENTRIES

The link **WebCT.com** leads
to the homepage of the company who makes this course management system. Its site contains various learning resources. It also offers bulletin board discussions with other students
taking WebCT courses at different schools. Within these communities you can share information, ideas, goals, and WebCT resources

Exiting WebCT

Some versions of WebCT have no logout button. If yours does not and you are working in
a laboratory or a place where other people have access to your computer, it is important to

quit your browser software completely when logging out. Otherwise, another person could take tests, submit assignments, send email, and post discussion messages using your identity. You must close all browser windows (not just the one that you were using to access WebCT), and you must also close the mail client to ensure that someone else cannot log in to your account. On a Macintosh, go to the File menu and select **Quit** or press **Command-Q** (⌘**-Q**). On a Windows machine, closing all of the browser windows and your mail program, such as Outlook Express or Netscape Messenger, will quit the program.

WebCT is very flexible, and courses may have very different appearances, icons, and so forth. Your instructor will decide on the structure of your course. But whatever that structure may be, there are certain navigational elements that are common across all courses.

The Course Homepage

Each course has its own **Homepage**, and you may find any level of information there, including links to other parts of the course. The accompanying figure shows you what one homepage looks like. Your course may have fewer or more icons, depending on the design your instructor or school has developed.

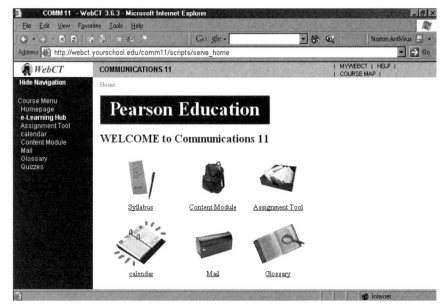

FIGURE 4.1 EXAMPLE WEBCT HOMEPAGE

The homepage is your base for navigation. It is the first page that you see each time you log in to the course (unless you have clicked on one of the links from the *myWebCT* page).

The Menu Bar

At the top of your browser window, you will see a menu bar, with links to *myWebCT*, **Course Map**, **Help**, and possibly **Resume Course**.

✔ *MyWebCT* returns you to the *myWebCT* page.

✔ **Course Map** allows you to see the course structure and available tools on one page. From the map, you can click on any of the linked course elements to go directly to any place in your course.

✔ **Help** appears on most pages of your WebCT course. Each Help link is context-sensitive, meaning that the help screen provided will be specific to the page or topic you are viewing.

✔ **Resume Course** allows you to return to the last place you visited in the course content.

The Navigation Bar

Depending on the settings created for your course, you may see a menu on the left side of your window. This left-hand navigation bar contains a Show/Hide Navigation toggle and a Course Menu section.

✔ The Show/Hide Navigation toggle allows you to turn the Navigation Bar off or on to expand the main window, or content area, of the course.

✔ The Course Menu provides access to course elements.

Breadcrumbs

Breadcrumbs, which appear in a list across the top of the content screen, show the sequential path of screens you have visited in the current session. You can return to any page in your list by clicking on the associated breadcrumb.

The Action Menu

After you enter a page of course content, you will see

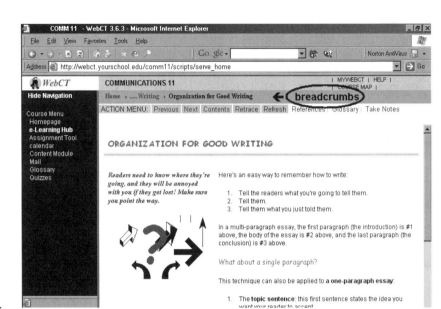

FIGURE 4.2   BREADCRUMBS AND OTHER NAVIGATIONAL MENUS

Tip

Avoid using your browser's *back* and *forward* buttons, which can have unpredictable results. Use the ACTION MENU or other links to navigate your course.

another navigation bar, the ACTION MENU. The action menu allows you to navigate the course content.

✔ **Previous** takes you to the previous page in the list of contents. If you are on the first page, this button will have no effect.

✔ **Next** takes you to the next page in the list of contents. If you are on the last page, this button will have no effect.

✔ **Contents** takes you to the Table of Contents for this section of the course, from which you can link to any page.

✔ **Retrace** allows you to visit the pages you have seen *in reverse order*. For example, if you began with page 3, and then read page 4, then page 5, Retrace would take you from page 5 to page 4 to page 3.

✔ **Refresh** allows you to return to a content page after you have viewed another link from the Action Menu (see tools listed below).

Depending on other tools your instructor might link to a content page, the Action Menu may also contain the following links:

Take Notes	allows you to take notes on the page of content you are viewing
Audio	links to any audio files associated with the content
Bookmarks	allows you to mark specific pages of content and then return to them by clicking on the bookmark link and then on the relevant bookmark
Chat	links to the live chat area of your course
Discussions	links to a discussion regarding the topic of the course content
Glossary	offers definitions and notes about terminology used in your course
Goals	lists learning goals that your instructor has set for the course content
Index	links to the index of your course
Mail	connects to the internal email system of your WebCT course
Quiz	links to any quizzes attached to the course content
References	presents a bibliography for the course content page and/or reference page numbers for assignments, readings, and so on
Search	offers a search tool to find particular words or phrases in the course content
Self-test	links to ungraded test questions about the course content
Video	links to any video files associated with the content.

Syllabus or Course Information

You can find information about your course in the course **Syllabus**. (Like most WebCT features, the availability of the syllabus or course information depends on whether or not your instructor has decided to offer it.)

Your syllabus may include information about the course requirements, books, instructor's contact information, and so forth.

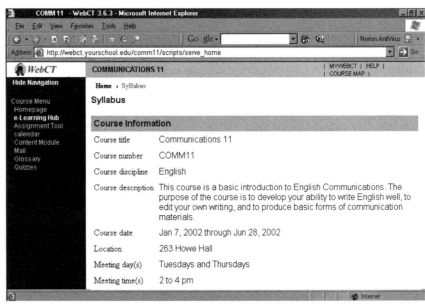

FIGURE 5.1   EXAMPLE OF A WEBCT SYLLABUS

Calendar

You will find calendars linked in two places: in *myWebCT* and within individual courses. As we mentioned in Module 3, you can access a calendar from your *myWebCT* page. You can switch this calendar to show information relevant to all of your courses or to each course individually.

You can also view your course-specific calendar by clicking on the **Calendar** link from the Tools page in your course (or wherever your instructor has placed the link). You can view your calendar data by day, week, or month.

If your instructor posts dates to the calendar, you can view them but you cannot change them. When you open the Calendar link, any new posts to the calendar will appear in a pop-up window from your browser.

You can enter your own information in the calendar, and it will be visible only to you. Private information is *italicized*, while public information is in regular typeface.

How to Enter Information into the Calendar

When you want to add information to your calendar, follow these steps:

✔ Click on the date, which is linked to open an input window.

✔ Click on **Add Entry**.

✔ Type in a summary of the event. This should be a short note that will appear in that date's box on the calendar, and should clearly indicate what the event is. (This element is required.)

Tip

If your instructor does not use the Calendar tool, you can use it yourself to ensure that you meet your deadlines. Make personal calendar entries for due dates from the assignment drop box, the syllabus, or other course information.

✔ Optionally, you may include a URL, if there is one relevant to the event.

✔ You may also add more details about the event. These will not show on the calendar itself, but will become visible when you open the page for the single day.

✔ Enter a start and stop time, if applicable.

✔ Click **add**

You will now see your entry summary appear on your calendar.

If you need to delete items from your calendar, click on the date, select an item from the day's events, and click **delete**. You can also edit your entries by choosing the **edit** button.

Module 6 Communication Tools

WebCT offers several tools that enable you to communicate both asynchronously (at different times, using **email** and **Discussion** boards) and synchronously (at the same time, using **Chat** or the **Whiteboard**).

Email

MAIL THIS

This tool allows you to communicate with your instructor and other classmates. The WebtCT mail tool will look familiar to anyone who has used email before. The main difference is that WebCT's email tool is internal to the system. (In other words, you can send mail only within WebCT and not out to others on the Internet.) Sometimes your instructor may allow you to forward messages to an external email account, such as Hotmail or Yahoo!. This communication works only one way; if you forward messages from WebCT, you may not reply back to WebCT.

RECEIVING NEW MAIL

The mail tool icon changes when you have new mail to read. Your email page will show your email folders and the number of messages in each, divided into read and unread messages.

READING MESSAGES

Each folder name (<u>All</u>, <u>Inbox</u>, <u>Outbox</u>, <u>Draft</u>, plus any other folders that you may have created to manage messages) is a link. If you click on the folder name, it brings up a list of messages in that folder.

FIGURE 6.1   MAIL TOOL OF WEBCT

SENDING MESSAGES

Clicking the **Compose Mail Message** link opens a new window. In this window you need to insert the user name of the person you're sending your message to. If you don't know the person's WebCT user name, you can browse the list of classmates by clicking the **Browse** button, selecting a name, and clicking **Done**. Then insert a subject and type your message.

You can send attachments by email as well. Under the **Attachments** part of the screen, use the **Browse** button to find the file (on your computer) that you want to attach. After you locate it, click the **Attach File** button. You will see your file name appear as a link. Your file name must be letters or numbers only; do not include spaces or special characters such as !, #, %, and so on.

Tip

If you know basic HTML tags, you can format your email messages in WebCT. If you do this, be sure to use the *Preview* button to see that your formatting appears properly.

ORGANIZING MESSAGES

Clicking on **Manage Messages** allows you to delete messages or move them between folders. You can also create new folders, or rename existing ones, to organize your messages into topics or however you see fit.

SEARCHING MESSAGES

Search allows you to search your mail by its different features. You can search for a certain word or phrase depending on folder location, status (read/unread), and criteria (date, sender, message number, body text, and so on).

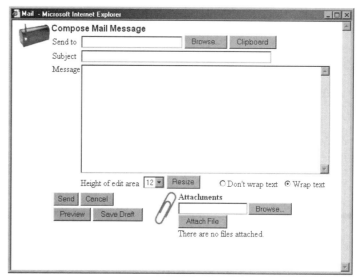

FIGURE 6.2   COMPOSING AN MAIL MESSAGE IN WEBCT

Discussion Boards

The **Discussion** area of WebCT is a space for students and instructors to post messages of common interest. People often use this area of WebCT to discuss course materials, exchange tips, ask questions, and share documents. It is also the location for private group discussions, if your instructor requires small group work in the course.

After you click on **Discussions**, you will see a table listing all of the topic areas, the number of unread messages, the total messages, and the status (public/private/anonymous) of each topic, which determines the type of interactions allowed. A topic that is public can be accessed by anyone in the course. If it is also unlocked, anyone may both view and post to that topic. A locked topic is read-only. A private topic is not accessible by all members of the course; rather, the instructor has opened it to a specific subset of people within the course. If a topic is anonymous, users may post anonymously if they choose to. From this screen, you can open separate topics, post (send messages), search messages, or set your display options.

Topic Settings allows you to control how many threads (replies to a posted topic) per page to display

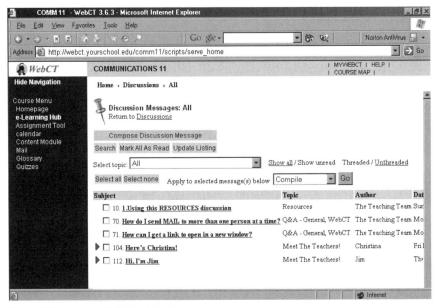

FIGURE 6.3   DISCUSSION BOARD LISTINGS

on your screen and the length of the subject line. Shortening the subject line can make it easier to view the full message line, including author, date, status, and attachments, without having to scroll to the right. To adjust the subject line, fill in the number of characters in the second text box and click **Go** to apply the change.

Once you have entered a specific topic, following are the options available to you:

Compose Discussion Message	write a message and identify it by topic
Search	search for content in the discussion space based on specific criteria you define
Mark All As Read	mark all the messages as read
Update Listing	update the listing to view messages posted since you logged in (including any you have posted since then)
Select topic	show the current topic and open a different topic area by clicking on it in the "Select topic" pull-down menu
Show all/Show unread	toggle between showing all the messages in a topic to showing only those you have not read
Threaded/Unthreaded	toggle between seeing messages and their replies in a nested format (threaded) and messages listed in the order they were received (unthreaded)
Select all	select all of the messages in a topic for some action
Select none	de-select any previously selected messages in a topic

READING MESSAGES

All messages are displayed by default. For those messages that you have not read, the label **NEW** appears to the right of the message's subject line.

To view all messages, read or unread, click on **Show all**. (If "Show all" does not look like a link, this option has already been selected.) To view only unread messages, click on the **Show unread** link. (If "Show unread" does not look like a link, this option has already been selected.) To read a message, click on the hyperlinked subject. If you see a paper clip, click on it to read the attachment.

REPLYING TO A MESSAGE

After you have opened a message, you can reply.

✔ To respond to a message without including any of its text, click on **Reply**.

✔ To respond to a message and include its text, click on **Quote**.

✔ To keep a copy of the message on your computer, click on the **Download** button.

COMPOSING MESSAGES

✔ To compose a new message, click on **Compose Discussion Message** button.

✔ A new window will appear, into which you must type in the following information:

• **Topic.** State where the message will be posted. (*Topic* is a folder. The *Compose Message* window includes a drop-down menu where the topic may be entered. If no topic is selected, the message will be posted to the default topic, *Main*.)

• **Subject.** Enter a summary or title for your message.

• **Message.** Type what you want to say.

• **Height of the edit area.** You can adjust the number of visible lines of your message. Click **Resize** after you have selected the number of lines from the pull-down menu.

• **Don't wrap text.** Display your message as one long line—that is, do not end this line, do not move to the next line.

• **Wrap text.** "Wrap" the text to the next line when it gets to the right of the input box.

- **Preview.** Review your message and edit it before it is placed in the discussion topic.
- **Cancel.** Cancel your message.
- **Post.** Place your message in the discussion topic. (This action cannot be reversed or the message deleted, except by an instructor.)
- **Browse.** You may attach files to your posts. Click **Browse**, which will provide a view of your computer's file structure. Under the **Attachments** part of the screen, use the **Browse** button to find the file you want to attach. After you locate it, click the **Attach File** button. You will see your file name appear as a link.

Chat

The Chat tool allows you to have conversations with classmates in any of your WebCT courses or even in other WebCT courses hosted on your school's server.

In the chat area, there are six "rooms," or areas, where you can chat. Four of these rooms may be labeled by the course's instructor, and the conversations that occur in them are logged and visible to the instructor. There is one general chat room for the course you are in now, and one general chat room that connects with students in all courses on the server. These two rooms are labeled "General Chat for [course]" and "General Chat for All Courses." These labels cannot be edited, and the conversations contained within them are not logged. Typically, your instructor will designate specific activities for the first four rooms, such as scheduled meetings, virtual office hours, collaborative projects, and so forth.

To enter a room, click on it. A space will open, as shown in Figure 6.4. The column on the right displays the user names for people who are in a room. You can send a message to the chat room by typing it in the message box at the bottom and pressing the **Enter** or **Return** key on your keyboard.

You can send private messages by clicking on a name or names in the **Current Users** box and then typing in what you want to say. You will see a confirmation on the screen that you sent a private message. Clicking again on those same names will deselect those users, and your next message will go to everyone in the chat room. By default, messages are public.

You can send a link to a Web page for your classmates by clicking on the **Send URL** button. Type the URL into the box and click the **Send** button. (You must include **http://** with the URL.)

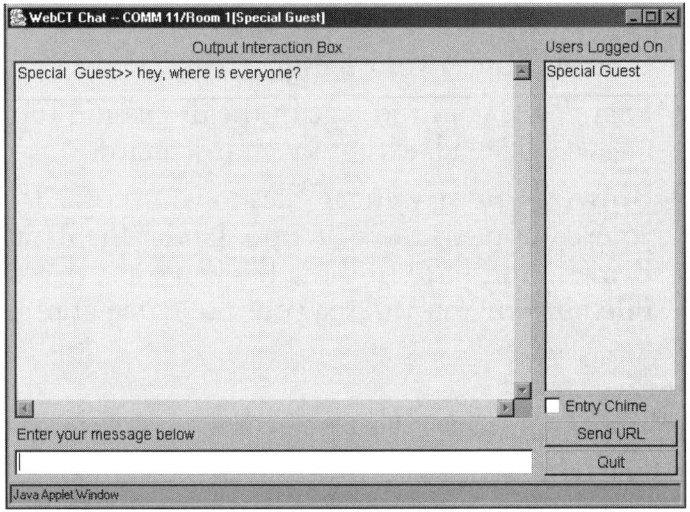

FIGURE 6.4 A CHAT ROOM IN WEBCT

Tip

Remember that your words in a chat room, discussion area, or email become public. Use humor, anger, or anything else that might be misinterpreted very carefully!

If you receive a URL, you can decide whether to accept it by clicking the **Okay** button. If you do accept it, the Web page will launch in a new window.

Four of the chat rooms are logged (all but the two general chat areas), so even though your chat may be "private" in the sense that you are restricting it to only some classmates, your instructor can view a record of the chat later.

To close the chat window, click the **quit** button.

Whiteboard

The **Whiteboard** tool allows you to share a real-time drawing and graphics board with users of your course. To open the **Whiteboard**, click on its icon, then **Start Whiteboard**.

    Whiteboard's drawing tools (see the accompany figure) are similar to what you'd find in other drawing programs. When you are in Whiteboard, placing your cursor over any of the tools will bring up its description in the **Information** box in the lower right part of your screen. (In the figure, the hand-shaped cursor is over the "Text" tool.)

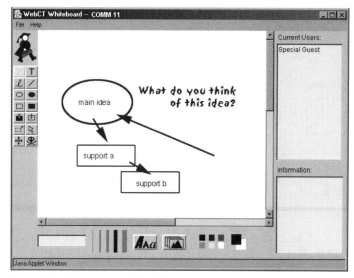

FIGURE 6.5   WHITEBOARD IN WEBCT

WebCT offers several ways for you to submit your work, take tests and quizzes, and complete course evaluations.

Assignment Drop Box

The assignment drop box allows you to submit work you have completed in a document while offline, such as a word-processing document, a spreadsheet, or any other format your instructor has designated. Depending on the configuration of your course, you may find **Assignments** linked on the Homepage and/or on the Course Menu.

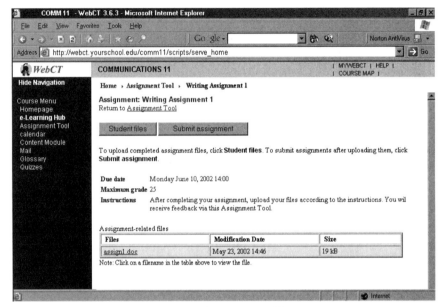

FIGURE 7.1   AN EXAMPLE OF AN *ASSIGNMENT* SCREEN IN WEBCT

VIEWING AN ASSIGNMENT

To **view** an assignment, follow these steps.

✔ **Step 1.** Locate the **Assignments** icon and click on it. The Assignments screen appears.

✔ **Step 2.** Click the linked name of the assignment you want to view (the link is underlined). If the name is not underlined, the assignment is not available. The *Assignment Instruction* screen appears, displaying the due date for the assignment, instructions for the completion of the assignment, and its maximum possible grade.

✔ **Step 3.** The *Assignment Instruction* screen also lists links to assignment-related files, if available. You can view them online if the format is viewable in browsers, or download them to open with the appropriate software.

SUBMITTING AN ASSIGNMENT

To **submit** an assignment, follow these steps.

✔ **Step 1.** Click **Student Files**, then **Upload**. Find the files on your own computer using the **Browse** button, and then click **Upload**. You can submit more than one file at a time if there are multiple files associated with your assignment. However, these files must be uploaded and submitted *at the same time* and not at different logins, since in most versions of WebCT submitting an assignment locks that tool until the instructor resets it. Uploading and submitting are two different actions; the

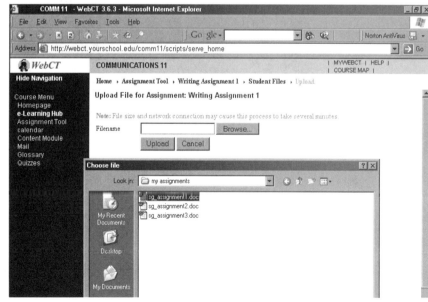

FIGURE 7.2   THE UPLOAD TOOL FROM THE *ASSIGNMENT* SCREEN

files must be uploaded **and** submitted for your instructor to receive your assignment. Remember to give your files names that contain no spaces or special characters such as punctuation, other than the underscore.

✔ **Step 2.** When you are ready, press the **submit** button. You will see a confirmation that your assignment has been sent. You may also receive an email confirmation of your assignment if your class's version of WebCT is configured to send one.

Self-Tests

Self-tests help you understand the course materials, but they are not recorded in your grade records. You can link to self-tests via the Action Menu. Clicking on the **Self-Test** link takes you to a multiple-choice test that will give you immediate feedback to your answers.

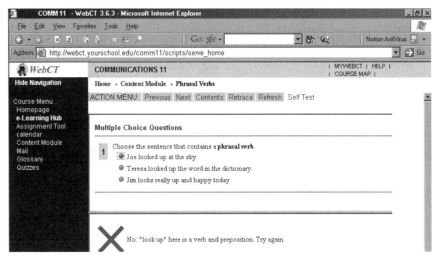

FIGURE 7.3   AN EXAMPLE OF A WEBCT SELF-TEST

Quizzes

Quizzes can take many forms in a WebCT course. They can contain essay, multiple-choice, fill-in-the-blank, or matching questions—or any combination of these question types.

Generally, the quizzes are scored, either automatically or by your instructor, and then stored in My Grades (See page 44.).

You can link to quizzes in WebCT from:

✔ Your *myWebCT* page

✔ The left-hand navigation bar

✔ An icon on the course homepage, or other organizer page

✔ A quiz link in the Action Menu of a Content page

ACCESSING A QUIZ

You can link to an available quiz from either a content page or from the quiz menu. If the quiz title is not linked, it means that it is not available to you. You will also see other information about the quiz.

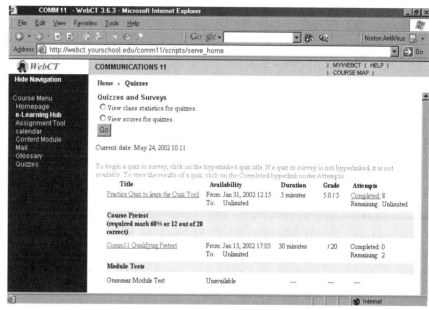

FIGURE 7.4　A QUIZ LISTING PAGE

✔ **Quiz Title.** The quiz topic

✔ **Availability.** The starting and ending dates for the quiz

✔ **Duration.** The amount of time you have to complete the quiz

✔ **Grade.** The total number of points assigned to the quiz

✔ **Attempts.** The number of times you may take the quiz. In this column, you will also see how many attempts you have already completed and how many are remaining.

Clicking on a linked quiz title will bring up an instructions page. (These instructions, similar for each quiz, offer reminders about how to take a quiz in WebCT. They are not written by your instructor.) Read the instructions carefully and completely. (Some instructions appear below the Begin Quiz button). The first paragraph of the instructions tells you whether or not you will get all the questions at once or one at a time, as well as whether or not you are able to return to questions after you have answered them.

When you are ready to begin, click the **Begin Quiz** button. Clicking this

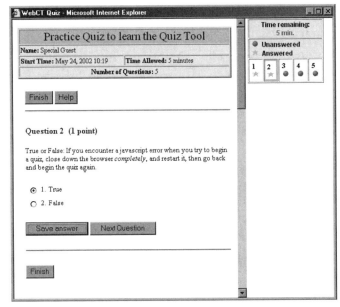

FIGURE 7.5 A QUIZ IN WEBCT

button starts the timer on your quiz. (Some quizzes are proctored and require a special password before you can begin. If so, you must enter your password before clicking the **Begin Quiz** button.) Be very certain that you do not click Begin Quiz until you are ready to take it. If you click Begin Quiz and then close the quiz window, the timer continues to run. If your instructor has allowed only one quiz attempt and has placed a time limit on the attempt, you may find that you are unable to take the quiz when you return to it.

ANSWERING QUESTIONS

✔ **One Question at a Time.** The next screen will show you the first quiz question. As you answer each question, you will see the **Save answer** button at the bottom of each quiz question. This button is very important! You must click on it after each answer. Clicking **Save answer** not only saves your work, but it updates the timer to the actual time remaining. After you have saved your answer, click on the **Next Question** button. If your quiz allows you to visit questions more than once, you can click through all the quiz questions to return to an earlier one. Be sure to press **Save answer** again if you change an answer.

✔ **All Questions at Once.** If all the questions appear at once, you must scroll down the page to get to them all. Remember to save your answers as you go. When all the questions appear at once, you may go back and change your answers. Don't forget to save your answer again after you have changed it.

ANSWER CONFIRMATION

Whether the quiz questions appear all at once or one at a time, you will see a box in the upper right hand corner of the quiz area called the **question status area**. At the beginning of the quiz, this box shows a red dot next to each question number. Whenever you save an answer, the red dot turns into a green star. The green star does not mean you have answered correctly or incorrectly. It indicates only that the computer has saved your answer. After you have saved a question, be sure the red dot has turned into a green star before continuing to the next question. (If a green star does not appear, it means your answer has not been saved. Press the **Save answer** button again in that case.)

Tip

If all the questions appear at once, be sure that you wait until the entire page loads before you begin answering them. If you do not, you may miss some quiz questions or not be able to save some answers.

THE TIMER

If your quiz is being timed, a timer will appear at the top of the question status area. This timer will count down and refresh itself every time you save an answer. In some cases, the instructor may have set the quiz so that you cannot submit your quiz after the timer has run out. In other cases, you may submit it, but your quiz will be recorded with a message that you took more than the allotted time to complete it. If you take a long time on one question, remember that the timer is not being refreshed. It's a good idea to keep track of time with your own clock or watch as well as with the quiz timer.

SUBMITTING THE QUIZ

Once all the questions have green stars and you are satisfied with your answers, you are finished with the test and ready to submit it for grading. At the top and the bottom of the page you'll find a **Finish** button. When you are done with your quiz, click on either of these buttons. **Important note:** You must click on the **Finish** button or your quiz responses will not be submitted.

After you've clicked on the **Finish** button, the computer will ask you if you really want to submit the quiz for grading. Click the **OK** button to submit the quiz; click the **Cancel** button to go back to the quiz.

SEEING YOUR GRADE

WebCT may automatically grade some types of tests and quiz answers, such as multiple-choice, matching, or short fill-in-the-blank type answers. You must click on the **View results** button to see your score. (The View results button may not appear at all, depending on the instructor's settings.)

In some cases, especially for essay or paragraph-type questions, the instructor will need to read and evaluate your answers. In this case, your grade will not be available until your instructor has reviewed your work.

Anonymous Surveys

Your instructor may request information from you anonymously. In this case, there will be an "anonymous survey" link on your Quiz page. This link is often used to get course or instructor evaluations or other types of information when the instructor does not need to know the identity of the student.

The format of anonymous surveys is the same as for quizzes, with multiple-choice, essay, or other types of questions possible. However, no score is required or available and the instructor has no way to know how a particular student answered, so surveys are truly anonymous. The instructor will see, however, how many students have completed the survey.

WebCT allows you to track your progress in your course by keeping records of which course content pages you have viewed, what quizzes you have taken, and so forth. As with other features of WebCT, your instructor decides on the availability or format of some of these items.

My Grades

WebCT allows you and your instructor to track your grades. Clicking on the **My Grades** button will give you a table of quizzes and assignments, along with any grades WebCT and your instructor have given you. The top part of the table will tell you the name of the quiz or assignment and its maximum grade or value in the course, while the bottom part will show you your actual grade.

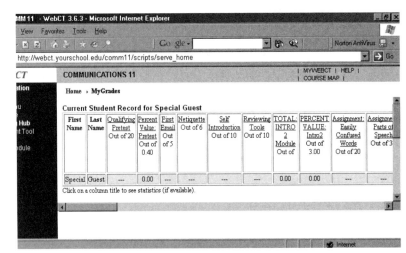

FIGURE 8.1   A MY GRADES TABLE IN WEBCT

YOUR SCORES COMPARED TO THE THOSE OF THE CLASS

When quiz or assignment titles are linked, you will be able to see how well you did compared to the rest of your class. You will not see specific grades for other students, of course, but a summary of how they did on the quiz or assignment. When you click on a linked title, you will see the total score possible, the highest and lowest grades, the average and midpoint (mean and median) grades, and the number of students who completed the quiz or assignment. There will also be a graph with the range of scores for an assignment or test, as well as how many people scored within each range.

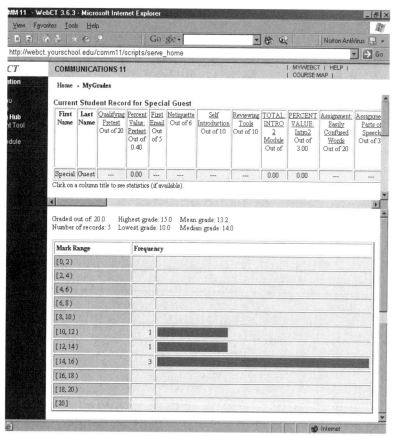

FIGURE 8.2   EXAMPLE GRAPH OF CLASS SCORES

My Progress

The "My Progress" section of WebCT allows both you and your instructor to see which pages within the WebCT course you have visited.

The *My Progress* screen has three areas.

✔ **Student Profile.** This area shows your name, User ID, date and time of first and most recent logins, total number of times you've logged in to the course, and the last page you visited. You will also see a link here that says <u>Show history of content pages visited.</u> Clicking this link will show you the when you visited all the pages you have viewed.

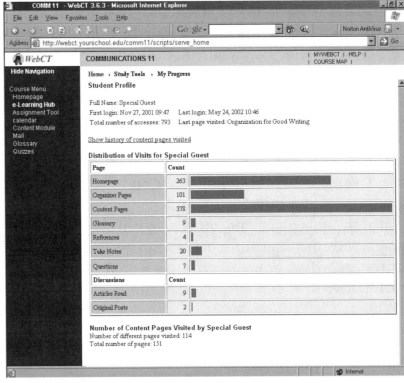

FIGURE 8.3 THE MY PROGRESS SCREEN IN WEBCT

✔ **Distribution of Visits.** This area shows you what kinds of pages or areas of the course you have seen.

✔ **Number of Content Pages Visited.** This part of the page tells you the number of different pages you have visited and the total number of pages in the course.

Search

The WebCT **Search** tool works like other types of Web search engines, except it searches only your course site for the word or phrase you want. To use **Search**, follow these steps.

✔ **Step 1.** Click **Search** on a course tool page or the **Search** link in the Navigation bar. The **Search** tool page will appear.

✔ **Step 2.** Identify what area of the course you'll search, and what you'll look for. From the Search drop-down menu, located in the top frame of the Search page, select how much of the site's text content you would like to search. You can choose from the following.

- **All.** Search everything in the course
- **All Content Module Text.** Search through the text contained in the course contents
- **Content Module Table of Contents.** Search only the headings and subheadings in the table of contents

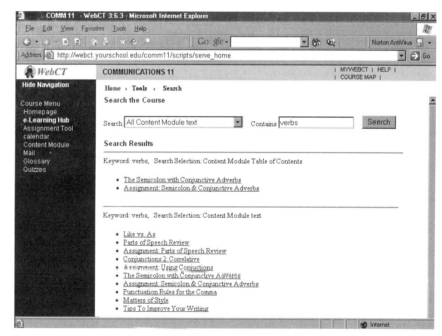

Figure 9.1 The Search Screen in WebCT

- **Headings in Content Pages.** Search only the headings contained in the course content pages
- **Discussion articles.** Search discussion postings

✔ **Step 3.** In the box next to **Contains**, type the word or phrase you wish to find.

✔ **Step 4.** Click **Search**. If the word or phrase is found, links to those pages will appear in the lower frame of the Search page. Click a link to go to a particular page, which will appear in a new window If the object of your search is not found in any of the areas you specified, *"No matches found"* will appear in the lower frame of the **Search** page. You may search for the item again and change the scope of your search (or check your spelling and try again).

Take Notes

The **Take Notes** tool acts like an electronic notebook. When you click on this link from the Action Menu of a content page, you will see a pop-up window in which you can write notes. When you return to that content page later, you can review your notes. Your instructor or other students cannot see your notes.

There are five buttons at the top of the *Notes* screen (six, if the Add button appears).

✔ **Close.** This closes the **Notes** window.

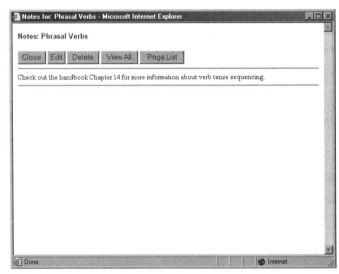

FIGURE 9.2   THE NOTE-TAKING SCREEN

✔ **Add.** This allows you to add a new note. (This button appears only if you have no notes attached to a page.)

✔ **Edit.** Add to, or change, existing notes. (This button appears only if you have already entered notes for a page.)

✔ **Delete.** This button deletes all the notes for the associated content page. When you press this button, you will be asked to confirm that you want to delete your notes.

✔ **View All.** Clicking this button shows you a listing of your notes, sorted by their associated content pages. There is a toggle to go back to the main *Notes* screen from this view.

✔ **Page List.** This option displays all content pages contained within the course, regardless of whether there are any notes associated with them.

Compile for Printing

The Compile tool may be available from several areas of a WebCT course. If there is a Compile link or icon available from a tool page or on your course menu, you can use it to compile content pages from your course for printing or to save on your computer.

To compile content pages, click on the **Compile** tool. A linked table of contents will appear, along with three buttons: **Compile**, **Select all**, and **Select none**. To compile content pages, you must first select which pages to compile. If you want to compile the pages for the entire course, you can use the **Select all** button to check all the pages listed. (Use **Select none** to uncheck them.) Then click **Compile**. This will open a new window with the compiled content in it. You can then save this file to disk or print it. **Important note:** Compiling large amounts of course material can take a long time, depending on the size of the file and the speed of your connection.

Tip
You can copy your notes from the *Take Notes* screen and paste them into a word processor document or an email message using keyboard short-cuts. For a PC, use Ctrl-C to copy and Ctrl-V to paste. You can use Ctrl-P to print. If you are on a Mac, use Command-C (⌘-C) to copy, Command-V (⌘-V) to paste, and Apple-P (⌘-P) to print.

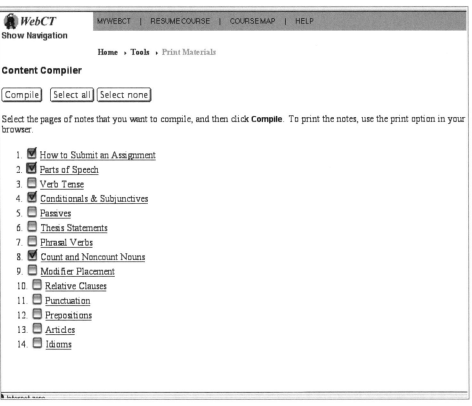

FIGURE 9.3   THE COMPILE SCREEN FOR COURSE CONTENTS

You can also compile **Discussion** messages. Go to the **Discussion Tool**. At the top of the main page, you will see a drop-down menu, for which the visible item is **Compile**. Select which messages you want to compile for printing or saving, and then click **Go**.

Other WebCT tools that allow compiling are email, notes, and calendar.

Image Database

Your instructor may provide one or more databases of images as part of your course content. Choose the appropriate database by clicking on its linked title. In the next screen, you will see a series of buttons and menus at the top that will allow you to choose how you want to view and search the images.

✔ **Show all.** allows names and descriptions of all the images to appear on the screen.
✔ **Search.** This pull-down menu allows you to choose *all images* or just *listed images*. (If you have already performed one search and want to search only the subset of images you retrieved, click on *Listed Images*.)
✔ **Criteria.** Lets you search by *key words*, *creator*, *file name*, *type*, or *description*.
✔ **Comparison.** Lets you choose the criteria used for searching.
✔ **Value.** Enter the term you are looking for. Then click the **Search** button.

A search must be performed by selecting the **Criteria** from the first drop-down menu (described earlier) and then the **Comparison** from the second drop-down menu (such as contains, equals, starts with, and so on). Next enter the appropriate entry in the text box marked **Value**.

For example: Creator (**Criteria**) → Starts with (**Comparison**) → J (**Value**.) This search would return a list of all images where the name of the creator begins with the letter "J". For another example: Key word (**Criteria**) → Contains (**Comparison**) → Michelangelo (**Value**.) This search would return all images that have Michelangelo associated with them as a key word.

Of course, you can browse through the images. There may be a thumbnail image with a link that says **View Image**. Clicking this link will bring up a new window containing the full-sized image. There is also a description of each image, including key words (which have been entered by the creator of the image database), the file name, the title of the image, and a description.

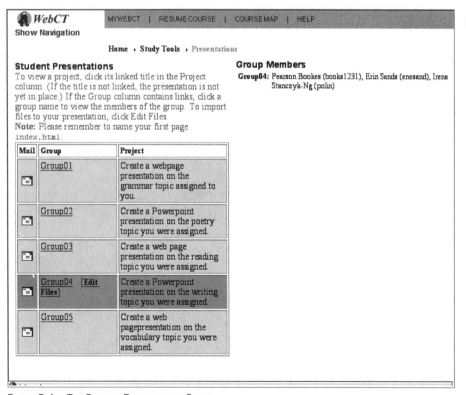

FIGURE 9.4 THE STUDENT PRESENTATIONS SCREEN

Student Presentations

WebCT not only delivers course material, but also allows you to create materials to share with your instructor and other students. The Student Presentations tool allows you to

✔ Create a linked set of HTML files
✔ Edit the HTML
✔ Let other students edit your HTML
✔ View other students' presentations

The files in your presentation will not be visible to your instructor and other members of your presentation group until you create a file called **index.htm** or **index.html** and add it to your presentation. This file will be the starting point for your presentation, and once you create it, a link will appear beside your presentation group's name, giving all members of your class a chance to view your presentation.

Student presentations require that you create HTML (Web) pages. It is outside the scope of this book to teach you how to do this. However, there are many websites and books, as well as free software, that show you how to create Web pages for uploading to your presentation site.

Student Homepages

Student Homepages allow you to

✔ Create a personal Web page within your WebCT course
✔ See a list of students who have homepages
✔ Link to other student homepages

The Student Homepage tool has an interface that allows you to create homepages without HTML. You can use this interface to choose pre-made banners or to upload your own.

Student Tips

Your instructor may provide a series of tips that will help you use your WebCT course more effectively. If your instructor has enabled **Student Tips**, you can view a "tip of the day," page through a list of the tips one at a time, show all the tips, and turn Tips on or off. A *tip of the day* will appear each time you log in unless you turn this function off. If you turn Tips off, you can still access the tips using the icon or link to the tool.

Glossary

If your instructor has set up the Glossary Tool, certain words in your course will be linked. When you click on a linked word (it is a different color and underlined, like any hyperlink in a Web page) from a content page, a small window will pop up with a definition or other notes about the word or phrase. Within this window you

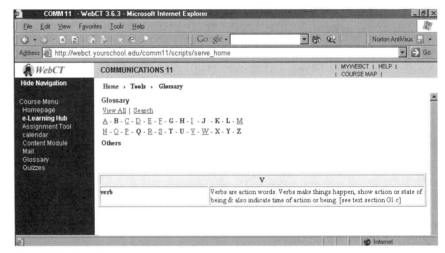

FIGURE 9.5 THE GLOSSARY TOOL

can go backward and forward alphabetically through the glossary items, or close the window.

You may also have a **Glossary** link from one of the tool pages. Clicking on its icon will bring up a window with the alphabet displayed. Any letters that have listings will be linked. Clicking on the letter will bring up the listings for that letter. You can also **View All** listings or **Search** through the listings.

CD ROM

CD-ROM is a WebCT tool that allows you to access CD-ROM media content in your WebCT course. You will need to configure your CD-ROM tool to specify where your CD-ROM drive is located on the computer you are using. On a Windows-based machine, this is typically drive D or E, on a Macintosh, it is the name of the CD-ROM.

To configure the CD-ROM tool, be sure the CD-ROM you will use is in your computer. Click **CD-ROM** on the course homepage to open the *CD-ROM Configuration* screen. You will then type the CD-ROM's location. For example, if the files are located in the root folder of the CD-ROM—that is, not in a subfolder-type D:\ or the letter your CD-ROM drive has been assigned. If the files are located in a subfolder on a compact disc named *Videos*, for example, you will type D:\Videos on a Windows machine with a CD-ROM Drive D.

If you do not specify this information, WebCT will send copies of the files the instructor has uploaded to the server on to your computer. (This happens only if the instructor has uploaded the files.)

Student Tracking

Your instructor may track information about your use of WebCT. This information includes your name and User ID as well as when you first accessed the course, the date and time of your last access, the number of times you've viewed course material, and the number of discussion items you've viewed and posted. Some instructors use this material to evaluate your participation in a course. Some instructors may consider this information important. Remember that if you click on the **News** links from *myWebCT*, the tracking information will not be logged.

Module 10 Where to Go for More Help

WebCT Homepage

The corporate site for WebCT (**http://www.webct.com**) has the most recent news about WebCT, including upgrades, tutorials, and so forth. If you have questions or problems with WebCT that you cannot resolve by using the **Help** button or by consulting this book, you should go to the WebCT site.

If you don't find the information you are seeking there, you should use **Ask Dr. C** (**http://www.webct.com/ask_drc/viewpage?name=ask_drc_student**), or navigate from the homepage: Customer → Ask Dr. C → Students. Ask Dr. C is a discussion forum where you can look at questions others have posted, along with their answers, or post a question of your own. Always look through the previously posted questions for an answer before you post your question. You can also search the questions and answers on Dr. C. **Important note:** This service is for help with WebCT, not for help with questions specific to your own course or institution. The Dr. C staff does not have access to individual school servers.

Additional Internet Help Sites

Your school may have its own website and help information for WebCT. If you don't know where that site is located, ask your instructor or search from the homepage of your school's website.

Remember that websites change constantly, and a website can disappear or change its address. To find other WebCT online tutorials or websites, you can use a search engine and enter the term WebCT student tutorial.

Frequently Asked Questions about WebCT

WebCT.com lists complete answers to FAQs at this website:

```
http://www.webct.com/support/viewpage?name
=support_FAQ_Student
```

Other FAQs

Q: I'm trying to upload a file to the assignment drop box, but I keep getting an error message. What's happening?

A: Be sure your file name has no spaces or special characters, such as !, #, $, and the like.

Q: We uploaded our files to the Presentation area, but they aren't linked. Why not?

A: Your main file must be named **index.html** or **index.htm** for it to link properly.

Q: We uploaded our HTML files, but the images aren't showing up? Why not?

A: You must upload your images separately from your HTML files. In other words, if your HTML file refers to an image called **image.jpg**, you must locate that image on your computer and upload it to your presentation or homepage area.

Q: The Whiteboard and/or Chat programs don't work right. Why not?

A: Your browser must have Java enabled for the Chat and Whiteboard programs to function properly. (See the pages 6–8 for details on browser configuration.)

Q: I can't see my lecture notes and assignments in PDF (Adobe Acrobat) format. Can I fix this?

A: There are problems with viewing files created in Acrobat 4.0 using Acrobat Reader version 3.0. Upgrade your Reader to the latest version at **http://www.adobe.com**.

Q: I forgot my password/login. Now what?

A: When you first registered for the class, you may have entered a password hint. If you did, go to the Entry Page for *myWebCT*, and then type your WebCT ID in the box. Your login information will be sent to you by email.

    If you did not enter a login hint, you should talk to your instructor, who may be able to reset your password for you. Please note that your campus may have a help desk or other arrangements for login help, so check any online instructions on this subject.

Q: How do I log out of a WebCT session?

A: In some versions of WebCT, a **Logout** button will appear in the top right corner of your screen. For all other versions, you must quit your browser and email software completely to log out of your WebCT session.

Q: Why can't I connect to WebCT from home?

A: Your Internet Service Provider (ISP) may use something called a Proxy Server to access the Internet. This proxy server may prevent access to your WebCT course. Check your proxy server settings (in Netscape, go to Edit→ *Preferences*; in Internet Explorer, go to *Tools* → *Internet Options*). If there is a proxy server setting shown, you must temporarily disable it while you access WebCT. Do not delete it; you should re-enable it after your WebCT session.

Q: Why can't I connect to WebCT from work?

A: Some companies have blocking problems on their firewall that prevent connecting to non-approved sites. It is possible that the company firewall is not allowing you to reach your WebCT course.

Tip

Don't forget that the *Help* link is available on nearly every WebCT page in your course. It will give you context-sensitive help on the tool or item you need.

Index